Scholastic Phonics

AF088203

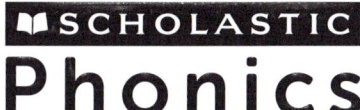

Choose a Hat

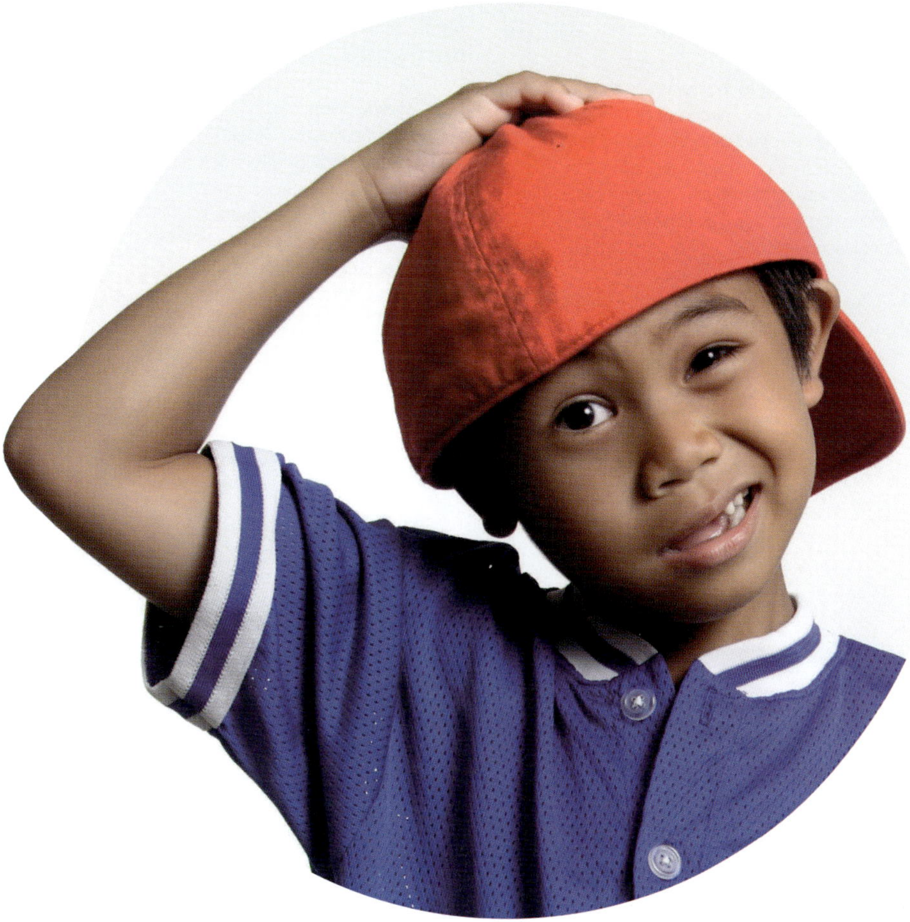

Published in the UK by Scholastic Education, 2023
Scholastic Distribution Centre, Bosworth Avenue, Tournament Fields, Warwick, CV34 6UQ
Scholastic Ireland, 89E Lagan Road, Dublin Industrial Estate, Glasnevin, Dublin, D11 HP5F

SCHOLASTIC and associated logos are trademarks and/or registered trademarks of Scholastic Inc.
www.scholastic.co.uk
© 2023 Scholastic
123456789 3456789012

Printed by Ashford Colour Press
The book is made of materials from well-managed, FSC®-certified forests and other controlled sources.

MIX
Paper from responsible sources
FSC® C011748

A CIP catalogue record for this book is available from the British Library.
ISBN 978-0702-32111-5

All rights reserved. This book is sold subject to the condition that it shall not, by way of trade or otherwise, be lent, hired out or otherwise circulated in any form of binding or cover other than that in which it is published. No part of this publication may be reproduced, stored in a retrieval system, or transmitted in any form or by any other means (electronic, mechanical, photocopying, recording or otherwise) without prior written permission of Scholastic.

Every effort has been made to trace copyright holders for the works reproduced in this publication, and the publishers apologise for any inadvertent omissions.

Author
Ann Hill

Editorial team
Rachel Morgan, Vicki Yates, Abbie Rushton, Jennie Clifford

Design team
Dipa Mistry, Andrea Lewis, We Are Grace

Illustrations
p10 QBS Learning

Photographs
Cover 2happy/iStock
p4 GabrielPevide/iStock
p5 Lucky Business/Shutterstock
p6 D Snyder/Shutterstock
p7, 24 gabriel12/Shutterstock
p8, 24 xavierarnau/iStock
p9 Valerie Loiseleux/iStock
p10 CW Pix/Shutterstock
p3, 11 Thomas Soellner/Shutterstock
p12–13 Mauricio Graiki/Shutterstock
p14–15 Christopher Ames/iStock
p16, 24 .shock/iStock
p17 Kateryna Kukota/iStock
p18 Aleksei Potov/Shutterstock
p19 Image Source/iStock
p20 Tomas Marek/Shutterstock
p21 Suthiporn Hanchana/Shutterstock
p22, 24 KELENY/Shutterstock
p1, 23 Geo Martinez/Shutterstock

SCHOLASTIC

Help your child to read!

This book practises these letters and letter sounds.
Point and say the sounds with your child:

- y (as in 'bumpy')
- ea (as in 'head')
- wh (as in 'wheel')
- oe (as in 'goes')
- ou (as in 'shoulders')
- y (as in 'fly')
- c (as in 'ice')
- ey (as in 'jockey')
- ou (as in 'you')

Your child may need help to read these common tricky words:

people's, the, their, who, they, are, one, into, to, would, there, was, were, your, of, different

Before reading
- Look at the cover picture and read the title together. Read the back cover blurb to your child.
- Ask your child: *What different sorts of hats can you think of? Why might people wear them?*
- Talk about the image in the magnifying glass.

During reading
- If your child gets stuck on a word, remind them to sound it out and then blend the sounds to read the word: h-ea-v-y, heavy.
- If they are still stuck, show them how to read the word.
- Enjoy looking at the pictures together. Pause to talk about the information.

After reading
- Talk about the images on page 24. What can your child tell you about them?
- Ask your child: *Does a firefighter need a soft hat or hard hat? What might happen when they are rescuing someone from a house?*
- Discuss what your child's favourite hat in the book was, and why.

Hard Hats

Hard hats (helmets) protect people's heads. This helmet is for ice hockey.

Players skate quickly. The hockey puck might fly up. A metal grid protects their faces.

puck

Who needs this helmet in their sport?
It is for jockeys. They might slip off their horses.

Jockeys' helmets are bright so people can spot each one in a race.

This is a firefighter. She goes into burning houses to rescue people. Things might tumble down on her head.

A plastic bit on the helmet protects her face from getting bruised or wounded.

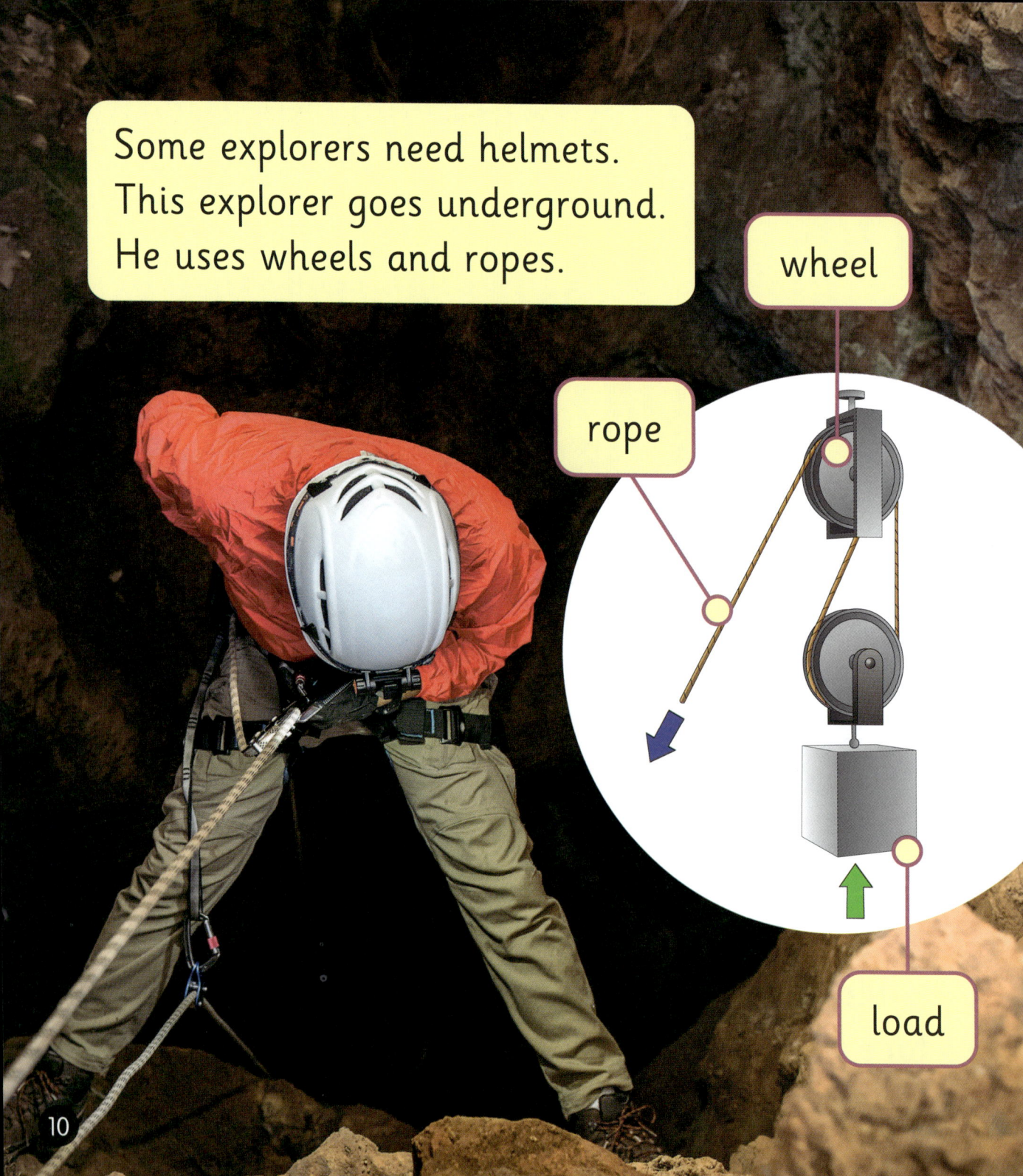

Some explorers need helmets. This explorer goes underground. He uses wheels and ropes.

wheel

rope

load

He crawls over boulders and finds grottoes and caverns. His helmet has a light so he can see in the dark.

Skydivers need helmets. A diver goes up in a plane, then jumps out. The helmet protects their head if they have a bumpy landing.

It protects them from the wind as they fly, too.

Why has this person got a helmet? He is a helicopter pilot.

The helmet would protect the pilot's head if there was a crash.

Soft Hats

Who needs a soft hat like this?

You would need one if you were a beekeeper.

The hat stops the bees from stinging her face. It reaches down to her shoulders.

beekeeper's suit

You need a hat in the sunshine. The sun burns. A sunhat protects your head and face.

A very wide floppy hat can protect your shoulders, too!

Fun Hats!

Some carnival hats are giant. They are heavy and must be hard to balance on people's heads.

Party hats are often pointy.

This funny hat hangs over the shoulders.

Hats come in lots of different shapes and sizes. Which hat would you choose?

Talk about it!